The Small Business Thrive Guide

How To Save Money and Thrive During Challenging Times

"Most great people have attained their greatest success just one step beyond their greatest failure."

- NAPOLEON HILL

It May Be Hard, But Don't Give Up

Running a small business isn't easy, even during the best of times. According to the United States Small Business Association:

- 30% of small businesses fail within two years
- 50% fail within five years
- Only 25% of businesses last 15 years or longer

Any small business owner will tell you that running a small business is challenging. You have to manage a thousand moving pieces, ensuring that you stay on top of cash flow, manage employee performance, sales, marketing, and many other factors.the success of your business is directly proportional to how much time and effort you put into it. Many owners struggle to manage all the different elements, and their business struggles as a result.

When circumstances get tough, running a business becomes an even greater challenge. Throughout the years, many events have occurred that placed a squeeze on businesses:

- The Great Depression
- World War I and World War II
- The Cold War
- The 2008 housing market collapse
- The 2020 coronavirus pandemic

During these difficult times, many small businesses folded under the pressure. They simply weren't able to keep going. Then there were the Titans that were forged from the fire or the warriors elect that knew how to think creatively and pivot. A successful business is built on the simple foundation of two things, supply and demand. Warriors and Titans recognize that the demand changes and they change with it to continue supplying the needs of the customers.

In the early 1920s, Prohibition prevented the sale of alcohol in the United States. As you can imagine, this made things really difficult for producers of alcohol.

But many companies adapted and came up with creative ways to save their businesses:

- Yuengling made ice cream
- Pabst made cheese
- Coors produced dinnerware
- Schlitz churned out chocolate
- Stevens Point Brewery went into the soft drink business

The point is that your business can make it through hard times. You'll need to get creative. You'll have to take decisive action. And you'll need to make tough decisions. But you can do it!

In his book *How The Mighty Fall*, Jim Collins wrote:

The signature of the truly great versus the merely successful is not the absence of difficulty, but the ability to come back from setbacks, even cataclysmic catastrophes, stronger than before. Great nations can decline and recover. Great companies can fall and recover. Great social institutions can fall and recover. And great individuals can fall and recover. As long as you never get entirely knocked out of the game, there remains always hope.

Don't give up. There is always hope!

In this small business survival guide, you'll discover effective steps to take that will help your business thrive in the midst of difficult times or when you feel like you've hit a wall, and your business is not growing. Keep in mind that these steps are not the easy way out, but they could be the difference between your business surviving, thriving or you having to close your doors.

Ready? Let's dive in.

Manage Your Mindset

If your business is struggling, it's absolutely essential to manage your mindset. When things get tough, it's really easy to enter a downward mental spiral.

You start thinking about all the circumstances that brought you to where you are. You second guess yourself, wondering whether you would be in a better place if you acted differently. You begin to doubt your abilities and whether you can ever succeed. The more you engage in these thoughts, the worse you'll feel. You remember every bad thing that every naysayer ever said to you when you told them about your business idea. You should know that if you are given a vision for a business, you do not need anyone to cosign your vision.

The vision was given to you not them. They will never understand nor accept the vision that you were given and taking action on a dream or goal is scary it's not for the faint hearted. Everyone will not be able to walk with you. Oftentimes the walk of an entrepreneur is a lonely one. Do not be concerned with this. Too many people in your circle can provide unnecessary distractions and cause you to miss key decision-making moments. I am not saying to leave everyone behind, I am saying to choose wisely who you allow to influence your decisions.

As you work to stabilize and turn around your business, it's important to maintain a positive mindset. Now, to be clear, this doesn't mean that you pretend everything is okay or bury your head in the sand. It means that you maintain faith in your ability to bring about positive outcomes. I for one am a strong believer in affirmations and goal setting. Write it down. Affirm it and make a plan of how to achieve it. Work on that plan every day.

A positive mindset also means that you are resolved to not give up. Keep striving to improve things and bring your business to a place of health. Have faith that everything will work out just as you expect it to. Keep working and whatever you do Do Not Give In to the fear that can grip you in uncertain times.

If you're struggling to maintain a positive mindset, remember that almost every great business leader has endured struggles similar to yours: it made them stronger. Diamonds are formed under pressure. Remember that.

- Thomas Edison failed thousands of times before he was able to develop a fully functioning lightbulb.

- Apple almost collapsed under bankruptcy when Steve Jobs was president.

- Bill Gates' first business was a complete and total failure.

- Henry Ford's first automobile business went bankrupt within a year.

In spite of all these difficulties, these individuals experienced great success. Why? **Because they persevered and were incredibly resilient.** Steve Jobs said:

> *I'm convinced that about half of what separates the successful entrepreneurs from the non-successful ones is pure perseverance. It is so hard and you pour so much of your life into this thing, there are such rough moments in time that most people give up. And I don't blame them, it's really tough.*

If you want your business to succeed, you need mental toughness. You must be able to persevere in the face of difficulty and keep going even when things look bleak. Get in touch with your inner warrior.

Follow these steps to overcome a negative mindset:

1. **Be Present.** It's easy to let negative thoughts take over in your mind without putting up a fight. If you're going to overcome these thoughts, you must be aware of what you're thinking. You need to be able to identify unhelpful mental patterns as they occur and stop them in their tracks.

2. **Be Affirming.** As negative thoughts arise, immediately affirm three positive thoughts. What we think about we bring about.

3. **Be Still.** After you've questioned and answered your negative thoughts, begin to silence them. Avoid letting the same thoughts steal your mental energy. You know they are only meant for harm. **Imagine that you have a remote and that you can mute your inner critic with the touch of a button. Press the button.**

4. **Meditate.** As you shut down your inner critic, fill the silence with positive, helpful dialogue. Regularly remind yourself that you are strong, are able to overcome challenges, and are growing in the midst of difficulty.

Learn Why You'll Want to Embrace Stillness and How to Do It

Stillness is simply being present in a peaceful and non-stimulating environment. If you're like most people, you're not taking the time to experience real stillness on a regular basis.

Most people are resistant to the idea of stillness for a couple of reasons:
They believe they don't have the time.
They're addicted to distractions and don't want to be alone with their thoughts.
See why practicing stillness is worthy of your time:

A more accurate perspective. When you're able to disengage for a few minutes, you can get away from your negative thoughts. You can step away from your life for a minute, and you have a better chance of seeing the truth. You're able to break away from your mental habits and experience increased clarity.
Your intuition can be heard. You can't hear your intuition if you're never still. It might be screaming at you, but you're completely oblivious to what it's trying to tell you. You become wiser if you experience stillness on a regular basis.
Less stress. When your mind gets a break from your busy day, you experience less stress. Of course, this enhances your sleep and overall physical and mental health.
Enhances your self-awareness. Stillness allows you to check in with yourself. You become more aware of your thoughts, aches and pains, and emotions. Instead of being engrossed in your habitual thoughts, you have the time and perspective to become more aware of yourself.

Stillness has many benefits that can greatly add to the quality of your life. If you're never still, you're missing out on a lot. It's easy to miss all the options and opportunities available to you if you never lift your head up above the noise. Stillness requires some time, but it's time well spent.

Stillness can be accomplished in different ways:

Meditate. Meditation is the most obvious way to practice stillness, but it's certainly not the only option. Meditation is a simple, but challenging, skill to master. Twenty minutes of meditation each day is an awesome way to practice stillness on a regular basis.

Turn off all of your devices and just sit, stand, or walk. Disengage from your computer, smartphone, TV, or other devices for a few minutes. Just look out the window, stare at the wall, or close your eyes for a few minutes. Focus on what you see, or just observe your breathing.

Strive to keep your thoughts to a minimum. Instead, focus on the information your senses are providing. What do you see, hear, smell, and feel?

Just a few minutes each hour can make a huge difference.

Spend time in nature. Cut yourself off from other people and anything manmade. Get out there with the trees, plants, and animals. Just enjoy your surroundings and give your brain a break for as much time as you can spare.

Be mindful. Mindfulness can be practiced anywhere. You can be mindful on the subway or in a business meeting. Keep your thoughts and attention on what you're doing and your surroundings. Avoid daydreaming, thinking about the past or the future, or anything that isn't relevant to what you're doing in the moment.

An overly stimulating environment can prevent the experience of true stillness, but it can greatly turn down the impact of the activity happening around you.

Schedule a little stillness into your life each and every day. It's that important. You might believe you don't have time for stillness, but that's the ultimate sign that you desperately need it.

Be still each day for as much time as you can spare. Your life will be changed in powerful ways.

As you push through problems and challenges, remember why you got into business in the first place.
What big problem were you passionate about solving? What

motivated you to take the risk of starting a business instead of playing it safe and taking a corporate job?

Seek to tap into the emotions and desires that originally pushed you to create your business. They can be the driving force that helps you make tough decisions and get things back on track. In my book Passion 2 Profit I talk about ways of identifying your profit making gifts.

"Some people dream of success, while other people get up every morning and make it happen."
– Wayne Huizenga

The key to developing any strength is practice. A weakness can even become a strength with practice. The challenge is getting yourself to practice regularly and intelligently.

The following strategies are important to remember when furthering the development of a strength.

- If you find your passion and develop a strength related to it, practicing will be fun. There's no reason to spend a lot of time on something that you don't truly enjoy. Find your passion first.

- Develop a goal. Having a goal is choosing to control the direction of your life. Otherwise, you're depending on luck to get wherever you end up. Review your goal daily.

- A goal should be specific, measurable, and have a deadline. To be most effective, all 3 characteristics must be present.

- Use meditation to learn to focus your thoughts and energy. The average office worker spends less than 2 hours per day actually doing constructive work. Do you focus better than the average worker?

- Learn to focus. It's relaxing for your mind and you'll get much more done.

- Use affirmations to replace negative self-talk. Simply turn the negative stuff around into something positive and supportive.

- Use visualization to see yourself already being successful. Experience your visions with all your senses.

- Measure your progress. This not only includes progress toward your goal, but also how well you're doing with reviewing your goal, your self-talk, level of focus, and more.

- Practice, practice, practice. The more you practice, the more you'll develop. But practice intelligently; have a plan and work on the most important things.

If you want to develop your strengths, you need to identify them and then practice. Anything that will help you spend more time practicing and practice more effectively is invaluable to your long-term development.

Clarify the Problem

Before you can identify a solution, it's important to first clarify the problem. Why is your business struggling in the first place? If you don't have clarity on the specific challenge you're facing, you won't know what steps to take to save your business.

Take some time to think about how you got to where you currently are. What happened that you didn't anticipate? What things went wrong? Often times you may not be able to see or predict a downward turn in business but these tools when applied might help.

Some common problems businesses face are:

1. **Market changes.** Economic factors, new technology, emerging competition, and many other things can cause the market to change. Survival requires the ability to adapt to changes as they happen.

2. **Failure to understand the target Client or market.** If people aren't interested in your product or service, there's a good chance you don't understand your Clients or market. Dig deep to understand what people truly want and what motivates them to buy. Consider hiring a marketing adviser.

3. **Poor pricing strategy.** If your prices don't match the Client demand, you simply won't sell much. It's crucial to understand what Clients are willing to pay, as well as where your product sits in relation to your competitors. You must check out your competition in business. It

helps you to grow and level up if need be.

4. **Insufficient funds.** Not having enough money on hand will quickly tank your business. You must pay close attention to cash flow, financing, sales, and more. Consider opening trade lines.

5. **Too much growth.** Growth is a good thing except when there's too much of it. If your business grows too fast, you might not be able to keep up with demand. Consider hiring staff. Remember that we are in the age of the internet. That thing that is costing you too much of your time to complete, you can hop on the internet and find someone willing and able to do that job and free up your time. Your time is too valuable, pay someone to do the things that you struggle with.

Identifying key problems within your business can be a painful exercise. No one likes to be reminded of ways they've failed. But if you want your business to thrive during challenging times, you must be able to put your finger on the primary problems.

If you're feeling sick and go to the doctor, what's the first thing they try to do? Determine what is causing the illness. Only then can the doctor prescribe the proper treatment. If the doctor has you start taking random medications in the hope that one will work, you likely won't get any better.

The same principle is true in business. **You must identify the cause of the problems before you can determine the proper solution.** The sooner you identify the problems, the better. If none of those suggestions spoke to your problem then you may need to hire a facilitator. They are worth their weight in gold trust me.

As Jim Collins wrote in *How the Mighty Fall:*

> *I've come to see institutional decline like a staged disease: harder to detect but easier to cure in the early stages, easier to detect but harder to cure in the later stages. An institution can look strong on the outside but already be sick on the inside...*

Focus on Your Clients

Before we get into details about specific actions to take, let's look at the big picture.

What is at the heart of every business, including yours? Clients.
I often say that we are not in the service business we are in the people business.
If you don't have Clients, you don't have a business. When deciding what actions to take to strengthen your business, always keep your Clients front and center. If you make changes that end up hurting your Clients, you're ultimately hurting yourself. You'll lose the people who are at the very center of your business. My business model has always been customer service centered. Look at the success of Publix, the coffee giant Starbucks and Chick Filet. Customer service is at the heart of their business model and they are thriving in every market. They have the heart of the customers.

Airlines are an example of what happens when you forget about your Clients. Over the last decade, airlines have gone to great lengths to cut costs and increase profits. Service declined and Clients were hit with various fees they never had to pay in the past.

The result? Clients are getting increasingly frustrated and fed up. It seems that everyone has an airline horror story. Flying, which was once seen as a luxury, is now often considered a necessary evil.

The moral of the story is to always keep your Clients at the top of the priority list.

Before making changes, consider how they will affect the Client experience. If Client experience is one of your key competitive advantages, be especially careful about changes.

If you destroy one of your competitive advantages, you may end up dealing a death blow to your business.

If you do make changes that will directly affect the Client, communicate those clearly. Explain to the Client why you have to make the changes and the outcomes you expect. The more transparent you are with your Clients, the more understanding they'll be.

Marketer Neil Patel is a good example of this kind of transparency. For a number of years, he made a particular software available for free. Eventually, however, the costs became too high and he was forced to start charging for portions of the software.

He sent a letter to his Clients, clearly explaining what was happening. He detailed his costs, making it clear that he simply didn't have the resources to continue making everything available for free. Then he laid out exactly what would happen moving forward.

You would be wise to follow Neil's example. Explain why changes are happening, when they will take effect, and how the changes will affect Clients.

I cannot stress enough how important great customer service is. Millions of people will go out of their way to patronize a particular business because they provide better customer service than the same business that might be much closer to them. It is a proven fact that poor client experience is the fastest way to lose a customer for life just as great client experience will gain you a loyal client as well as referrals.

During times of global crisis, it is especially important to keep the focus on Clients. People will remember the actions you take. If you seek to serve your Clients, even at the expense of profit, you will build up a huge amount of goodwill and loyalty.

For example, during the coronavirus crisis, many companies sacrificed financial gain for the sake of their Clients:

- Many educational companies made their resources free to parents who were suddenly forced to homeschool their children.

- **Audible** gave away free audiobooks for kids.

- **Moz** provided free courses on search engine optimization to help businesses strengthen their online presence.

- **Loom** offered significant discounts on their video recording platform so people could stay in touch with family and friends.

- **Bill.com** made their platform available for free for 90 days to anyone affected by the coronavirus.

All of these companies are losing out on potential profit by giving these things away for free. But Clients will remember the actions taken by these businesses and will be much more likely to support them in the future.

It's about building your brand by doing good for others, instead of focusing on the bottom line.

Bottom line: If you keep the focus on Clients, there's a much greater chance that your business will weather the tough times.

"The more you engage with Clients the clearer things become and the easier it is to determine what you should be doing."

- John Russell

Conduct A SWOT Analysis

If you want to succeed as a small business owner, you must be willing to honestly evaluate how things are going. You can't ignore problems. You can't just hope that things get better. You must take a long and hard look at your business and then make changes based on what you see.

A SWOT (strengths, weaknesses, opportunities, threats) analysis provides you with a framework for analyzing your business. It helps you identify what is and isn't working, spot potential growth opportunities, and prepare for external threats.

Let's look at each aspect.

Strengths

These are the things you have control over and are working well in your business. **Focus on and try to develop these areas further.** For example:

- Effective sales team
- Proprietary technology
- Proven marketing strategy
- Powerful systems/processes

- Strong Client base

Weaknesses

These are the things that aren't working well in your business. **Your goal is to change or eliminate these things so that they don't continue to damage your business.**

For example:

- Ineffective marketing strategy
- High production costs
- Low profit margin
- Poor Client retention
- Ineffective internal processes

Opportunities

These are external factors that have the potential to benefit your business. **The more you can capitalize on these opportunities, the more success you'll have.**

For example:

- New technology
- Less competition
- Fewer taxes
- New markets
- Improved economic environment

Threats

These are external factors that could possibly hurt your business. **Either avoid these things or adapt to them.**

For example:

- Increased competition
- Changing Client preferences
- Worsening economic conditions (recession)
- New regulations
- Significant technological changes

Performing a SWOT analysis is hard work. It's essential to be honest about the current state of things and acknowledge areas where you're struggling. This clear-headed analysis will help you overcome your weaknesses, capitalize on your strengths, and take advantage of unique opportunities.

S	W	O	T
Strengths	Weaknesses	Opportunities	Threats
What are your personal internal strengths that you can lean on to help you achieve your goals?	What are your personal internal weaknesses that you need to work on to achieve your goals?	What external opportunities such as resources, people, or training can you take advantage of to help you achieve your goals?	What external threats such as upcoming obstacles or contextual factors can you predict and mitigate to ensure you reach your goals?

Create Objectives and A Plan

Once you've done a SWOT analysis, take what you've learned and put it into action. Determine the objectives you'll pursue and create a plan for achieving those objectives. This will give you the clarity you need to move forward.

Start with your strengths. How will you double down on the things you're already doing well? Does your sales team have a high close rate? Focus on getting more prospects to the team. Do you have a large email list? Work on converting them from readers to buyers.

Then look at your weaknesses. How can you change, minimize, or even eliminate these areas? Is your profit margin low? Create a plan for reducing production costs. Do you have trouble keeping Clients? Develop a Client retention strategy.

Move on to opportunities. Is there a new market you can move into? Can you implement a new technology that will help you be more efficient? Determine the greatest opportunities for your business and the steps you'll take to capitalize on those opportunities.

Finish with threats. How will you avoid or adapt to those things that could hurt your business? Do you need to take steps to adjust to new Client preferences? Do you need to change your pricing strategy to keep up with the competition?

Remember to create both objectives *and* a plan for how you'll meet those objectives. It's not enough to say, "I want to increase my profit margin." You also need to determine the specific steps you'll take to make that happen.

Your objectives need to be:

- **Measurable**. You must be able to determine whether you've hit your objective.

- **Achievable.** Be realistic in your goal setting. Aim for things that you can actually achieve.

- **Timely.** Set a specific date by which you'll meet your objectives. This will give you a sense of urgency.

"Doing the best at this moment puts you in the best place for the next moment."
– Oprah Winfrey

Reduce Costs

If you want your business to survive and thrive during difficult times, you'll likely need to reduce your costs. However, **be careful and precise as you do this.** Cut costs too much and your business may have a hard time recovering. Cut costs too little and you won't free up enough cash to keep your business going.

Follow this process to reduce your costs:

1. **Start by cutting discretionary costs.** These are costs that aren't necessary to run your business. Business lunches is a good example of a discretionary cost. Yes, it may be helpful to meet clients over lunch, but it's not necessary. You can meet them over coffee or in your office and save quite a bit. Other discretionary costs include:

    - Coffee/tea for the whole office
    - The highest speed internet (switch to a lower speed)
    - Magazine subscriptions
    - Off-site events
    - Advertising
    - Consider whether a brick and mortar store is needed

2. **Next, look at ways you can reduce costs but still achieve the same outcomes.** For example:

    - Can you reduce travel costs by using videoconferencing technology?

- Can you cut IT costs by using less expensive cloud software?
- Can you reduce utility costs by finding ways to use less water or electricity?
- Get creative when looking at these costs.

3. **Next, consider your office space costs.** Your landlord may be willing to lower your rent or even create a new lease for you. Explain the challenges you're facing and the possible outcomes if you don't make significant changes. If your landlord won't reduce your rent, consider moving to a less expensive building.

    - If your business is small enough, you may want to think about running it out of your home, at least temporarily. This can significantly reduce insurance costs, taxes, utilities, and more.

4. **Also take a close look at your supply chain.** Some of your suppliers may be willing to give you discounts, especially if you've been a good Client and always paid on time.

    - If your current suppliers don't offer discounts, explore alternatives. If a new supplier offers you a discount, you may be able to leverage that with your current suppliers.
    - Explore supply on demand or drop shippers so that you are not stuck with unsold inventory.

5. **At some point, you'll need to think about reducing staffing costs.** This is hard for every business owner. No one wants to put someone out of a job or reduce

someone's income.

- However, if you want your business to survive, you have to be willing to make these hard decisions. Cutting staffing costs today ensures that you'll still have a business in the future.

- Before you lay people off, look for ways you can reduce employee hours or compensation. Obviously, you'll need to communicate clearly with your employees. Explain why you're cutting these things and how long you expect these measures to last. Consider a commission-based employment strategy.

- If a reduction in hours or compensation isn't enough, you'll have to reduce your workforce.
- I am a firm advocate that before you explore layoffs have a transparent team meeting. Ask the team to come up with ideas to save costs or pivot the spiral. I remember being a part of one such meeting for a multi-million dollar company that was in negotiations for a merger. The new company wanted a non-negotiable which was to perform abortion procedures along with the layoffs of about 30 % of the staff and on a last pitch effort we had a bare it all conversation with everyone and the secretaries and janitors came up with a million-dollar idea to save the company. You never know where your help will come from. **Be transparent**.

Cutting costs isn't a fun thing. You and your employees will have to make sacrifices. You'll have to give up perks and luxuries. But it's important to look at the big picture.

The actions you take today will produce results long into the future. Sacrificing in the present increases the chances of your business surviving for years to come.

"I attribute my success to this: I never gave or took any excuse."
– Florence Nightingale

Manage Your Cash Flow

Your cash flow is what will ultimately determine whether your business survives. Every month you have cash come into your business in the form of payments from Clients. You also have cash going out of your business for expenses like rent, supplies, and salaries.

Now, to be clear, when we say "cash", we don't necessarily mean actual cash. We simply mean money going into and out of your bank account. Hopefully that went without saying but just in case this is your first rodeo, cash means income/profits.

Not having enough incoming cash is one of the biggest reasons small businesses go under. When you run out of cash, you can't pay your bills, purchase supplies, or any of the other necessary tasks to keep things running.

This means you need to pay very close attention to your cash flow.

Here's a quick way to evaluate your cash flow:

1. At the end of the month, add up your total sales.
2. Total all purchases that you still must pay for.
3. Calculate the difference.

For example, let's say you have $10,000 in sales. You still owe $6,000 for purchases. Your cash flow is approximately $4,000. If you have negative cash flow, you'll need to make up the difference in the next month. The more you fall behind, the harder it is to make up the difference.

If you have accounting software, you should be able to create a detailed cash flow report relatively easily.

If you find yourself struggling with cash flow, you do have some options, such as:

- **You can sell assets to bring in additional cash.** For example, you could sell a company vehicle or a piece of machinery.

- **You can get a working capital line of credit.** You are given a set amount of credit from which you can draw when cash is tight and pay back when you have surplus cash. You only pay interest on what you borrow. For example, if you have a $10,000 line of credit and borrow $5,000, you only pay interest on the $5,000.

As much as possible, stay abreast of your cash flow. I recommend switching to a weekly profit and loss tally. How much did I earn? How much did I spend? What do I have left? Send out invoices in a timely fashion and follow up with Clients who fall behind on payments. Pay your own bills on time and try to plan accordingly for purchases. If you sell physical services map out a plan of how many products at what price do you need to sell in order to stay afloat daily/weekly/monthly/annually. Plan plan plan. Count the cash.

Cash really is king.

Meet With An Accountant

As you work to stabilize and strengthen your business, you would be wise to meet with a certified accountant. There are a number of reasons for this.

First, they can help you implement money-saving tax strategies. Taxes are complicated, especially when you're running a business. There are a number of specific actions you can take to reduce your tax burden.

For example, you can:

- Change the depreciation method used on your assets.
- Defer income to the following year.
- Restructure your business.
- Maximize expense deductions.

Because tax laws are so convoluted, many of these strategies are not intuitive. An accountant can help you know what actions to take. Please make note that all accountants are not created equally. Make sure to vet this person thoroughly before handing over your kingdom. You worked hard for this, and a bad accountant could bankrupt you.

Second, an accountant may be able to help you secure financial assistance from the local, state, or federal government. Because small businesses are good for the economy, many government agencies are willing to provide financial aid for struggling businesses.

For example, the Small Business Association offers low interest loans and grants to qualifying businesses. Some state and city government organizations also have relief programs designed to strengthen small businesses. An accountant can help you find and secure government funding for your business.

Finally, an accountant can help you think through critical financial decisions. Many business owners struggle to absorb all the financial details about their company. This is common and nothing to be ashamed of. However, if you struggle in this way, it can make it challenging to stay abreast of important numbers like cash flow.

An accountant can crunch all the numbers for you and then provide you with relatively easy-to-digest reports. They can also give you guidance as you make important decisions like what costs to cut. I recommend also using a great tracking software like Intuit for business payroll and spending.

Creativity is great - but not in accounting.
– Charles Scott

Use Low-Cost Marketing

Marketing is a double-edged sword. On the one hand, it costs money to get your company name out there. Obviously, money you spend on marketing can't be spent on essential things like payroll and bills. On the other hand, if you stop doing marketing, you connect with fewer Clients, which also decreases available funds.

So, what should you do when your business is struggling? Should you cut your marketing budget? Should you double down on marketing?

Answer: yes.

Use low-cost marketing to simultaneously cut your budget and increase your efforts. Traditional advertising methods such as television, radio, and billboards tend to be pretty expensive. You don't need to use these strategies to get in front of Clients. Other techniques can be just as effective at a fraction of the cost.

For example:

- Regularly ask your existing clients for referrals. If you've provided your clients with great service, they'll be glad to send people your way.

- Local business networking groups are a great way to connect with potential clients in your community.

- Trade fairs or business meetups allow you to connect with key individuals in your industry.

- Write guest blog posts for websites in your industry.

- Appear on podcasts that your audience listens to.

- Develop strategic business partnerships that foster cross-promotion (you promote them, and they promote you).

- Build an email list and then consistently send out valuable information to your subscribers.

- Sponsor local events (charitable, sporting, and more).

- Maintain a consistent presence on various social media platforms.

- Create highly targeted online advertisements. This can be done for just a few dollars per day.

- Develop a cold calling strategy and make calls each day.

- Develop relationships with influencers who may be willing to promote your products.

- Create an affiliate program that rewards those who promote your products.

- Host events or classes (locally or online).

- Offer to speak at local business groups, community colleges, libraries, and conferences.

- Create a YouTube channel where you consistently deliver valuable information.

- Run online contests using a platform like Gleam.io or King Sumo.

- Offer a free trial of your product and create a process to turn those free trials into paying Clients.

- Livestream from your workplace to show others what happens behind the scenes.

When it comes to marketing, you're only limited by your imagination. Get creative and step outside your comfort zone. Reach out to people you normally wouldn't. Thanks to the internet and smartphones, marketing is easier and cheaper than ever. Take advantage of the connected world in which we live.

"I knew that if I failed, I wouldn't regret that, but I knew the one thing I might regret is not trying."

– Jeff Bezos

What Baby Shark Can Teach You About Success

What makes Baby Shark so catchy? It's a children's song and a top 40 hit that appeals to kids and adults around the world. It has spawned dozens of variations and its own line of toys. It's been viewed more than one and a half billion times on YouTube.

By now, you've probably seen the video regardless of whether you have any small children at home. Maybe you've even danced along as the family of sharks goes hunting and cheered for the happy ending where everyone winds up safe.

There's plenty of unpredictable magic behind any internet sensation. However, you can tap into some of the ingredients that make these little sharks such a success, starting with these 3 basic principles.

The Value of Simplicity

The song is only 1 or 2 minutes long, and most of the lyrics consist of repeating the sound DO. Free up your time, save money, and reduce stress by getting down to basics.

Use these strategies to simplify your life:

Buy only what you need. Studies show that experiences rather than possessions contribute more to happiness. Develop a hobby instead of shopping for entertainment.
Clear away clutter. Take a look at the possessions you already have. Put aside things you can donate or sell. Owning less stuff means less time spent cleaning and maintaining it.
Be mindful. Forget about multitasking. Instead, focus on doing one thing at a time. You'll experience less stress and the quality of your work will increase.
Give thanks. Appreciate what you have rather than longing for more. Make a list of the things you're grateful for.

Set priorities. Figure out your values and what you want to do to live a meaningful life. Schedule your time so you can channel your resources where they'll have the most impact.

The Importance of Family

Baby shark sticks close to his parents and grandparents. The quality of your relationships plays a big part in determining how happy and productive you are. Surround yourself with love and support from the family you were born into or the one you create.

Try these techniques to strengthen your family bonds:

Talk more. Listen closely to each other. Describe your dreams and express your feelings. Help each other to feel valued and understood.
Eat family dinners. Sit around the same table for a meal at least once a week. If dinner is difficult to coordinate, make it breakfast or lunch.
Spend one on one time. In addition to family outings, plan activities that you can do separately with each child and your partner. You'll create a closer connection and lasting memories.
Share decision making. Giving each family member a voice in the process increases the enthusiasm for working towards shared goals. Vote on where to go for your next vacation. Let your child decide which homework assignment to complete first.

The Power of Repetition

Major accomplishments usually require many small actions. Repetition helps important lessons to sink in.

Follow these steps to make small changes with big results:

Clarify your thinking. Even when a subject seems basic, reviewing the matter may deepen your understanding or reveal new facets. You could wind up with a stronger business plan or a scarier shark costume.

Pick up new skills. Expertise is usually developed through extensive practice. Be persistent and strategic about building your core strength or looking for love.

Form positive habits. It's easier to make constructive choices when you make the process automatic. After a month of jogging each morning, it will seem like the natural thing to do.

Baby Shark is so much fun that it will make you feel safe to go back in the water. Let this children's song inspire you to simplify your life and create your own happy endings.

Be Persistent, Be Creative, and Pivot

What separates businesses that fail from those that thrive? Persistence and creativity. Successful businesses persist through challenging times and come up with creative solutions to difficult challenges. They don't give up in the face of adversity. Sometimes they even pivot to a completely different business model. Perseverance is key.

Polaroid is an example of a company that didn't approach problems with persistence or creativity. **They failed to pivot when it really mattered.**

As digital photography began to take over in the late 90's, Polaroid executives continued to insist that people wanted hard copy photos. They ignored the massive issue that was staring them in the face and wouldn't consider any other business model.

As a result, they were forced to file for bankruptcy in 2001. The once-great company was largely destroyed.

Yelp, on the other hand, used creativity and persistence to overcome difficulties. The service started as a platform for getting recommendations from friends. Even though they managed to get $1 million in funding, they couldn't seem to get much traction.

They noticed, however, that people enjoyed writing reviews of local businesses. They pivoted to focus on making it easy to write reviews and the rest is history.

Even in the worst circumstances, there are still options.

During the coronavirus pandemic of 2020, many companies pivoted in big ways:

- **Anheuser-Busch** began manufacturing hand sanitizer.
- **Hanes** started producing medical masks.
- **Lyft** used their huge fleet of cars to deliver medical supplies.
- **Ford** used its infrastructure to make ventilators and medical face shields.
- **Farmers Restaurant Group** shifted to delivering food supplies to Clients.

How can you pivot in your business, so you stay afloat and meet the demand of your clients?

There are numerous ways you can pivot your business:

1. **Utilize new sales channels.** If you run a brick-and-mortar business, consider also selling online.

2. **Segment your Clients.** 80% of your revenue comes from 20% of your Clients. Instead of trying to please everyone, focus on the 20%.

3. **Focus on a feature.** If you sell a product that has one particularly popular feature, focus much more heavily on that feature (like Yelp did with reviews).

4. **Change your revenue model.** Historically, journalism relied heavily on subscriptions for funding. As we've moved into the internet era, many have pivoted to relying on advertising.

5. **Change your pricing and positioning.** If you can't compete with someone on price, compete on quality, or vice versa.

6. **Adopt new technology.** New tech can help you reach more Clients. For example, if you're a tutoring company, using a platform like Zoom allows you to communicate with people virtually.

7. **Consider Investing in a Business Coach.** A great secret weapon when you have run out of ideas on how to grow your business is investing anywhere from a few hundred to a few thousand dollars for a great return on your investment from a business coach. They can provide you with fresh business ideas to help you pivot when needed. **I recommend A.I.Motivation but that's just me, pun intended.**

The reality is that every business will face challenges. Technology is constantly changing. The market is always in flux to some degree. New competitors regularly emerge.

These difficulties don't need to sink your business. Don't give up. Persistence produces success.

As Jim Collins said in *How The Mighty Fall:*

> *The path out of darkness begins with those exasperatingly persistent individuals who are constitutionally incapable of capitulation. It's one thing to suffer a staggering defeat – as will likely happen to every enduring business and social enterprise at some point in its history – and entirely another to give up on the values and aspirations that make the protracted struggle worthwhile. Failure is not so much a physical state as a state of mind; success is falling down, and getting up one more time, without end.*

If you fall, get back up. Again, and again. The formula for winning is just that simple. You must just get back up and begin again after each fall. Take the lesson from the fall!

Take Action Today

If you want your business to survive the storms, you must take effective action immediately. Avoid just trying to wait it out, hoping things will get better. As is commonly said, hope is not a strategy.

It is the doers who are successful: those who confront the challenge head on, map out a strategy for change, and begin acting on that strategy.

Habits of Ultra-Successful People

If you've ever known anyone ultra-successful, you know that they can appear to be a different breed. We're not talking about someone that's a straight-A student and goes on to make $250,000 per year. We're talking about people that win gold medals, become billionaires, or impact the entire world in some way.

These ultra-successful people are all unique, but they share many of the same habits.

Mimic these habits of successful people and become more successful yourself:

    1. Get up early. The vast majority of the most successful people in the world get up very early. They make great use of this time, too. They have a morning routine that often includes exercise and meditation or prayer.

    ◦ Try getting up an hour earlier and have a plan for using this time effectively. Do this for 30 days and evaluate the results.

    2. Practice self-discipline. Success requires work. High levels of success require doing work that most people aren't

willing to do. It takes self-discipline to do difficult things day after day.

◦ Work on your self-discipline each day. You have countless opportunities to do this. If you need to lose weight, throw out 25% of your lunch each day. When you feel like taking a break, force yourself to work for another 15 minutes.

3. Become action oriented. People with mediocre levels of success often like to plan, but they struggle to actually take any sort of action. Successful people take intelligent action. They are the masters of getting things done. They're also great at getting started on new projects.

4. Read daily. Reading saves years. Without reading, you're forced to figure out a lot by yourself. A book written by a competent author is like a mentor. The world is full of experts. Why try to do it all yourself? Stand on the shoulders of the world's all-time greats.

◦ Buy a good book and use the information in it. Life is too short not to take advantage of the expertise of others. Remember that it's not enough to read and understand the information. You must apply it.

5. Get clear on your goals. Ultra-successful people know exactly what they want. The average person does not. You can't make progress toward a goal if you're not aware of your goal.

◦ Decide what you want. Make a list and be precise.

6. Say, "No" to practically everything. Highly successful people avoid distractions much better than the average person. Many of us say "Yes" to almost every opportunity. Successful people say "No" almost all the time.

◦ Decline offers that don't assist you in the pursuit of your goals. Everything you do either brings you closer to, or takes you further from, your goals. Before agreeing to something, ask yourself, "How does this impact the pursuit of my goals?".

7. Persevere. The most successful people have a tenacity that most of us fail to demonstrate. We give up far too easily.

◦ Set goals that truly excite you. That will encourage you to continue when the going gets tough. Practice persevering when you want to quit. Learn how to grind and get things done. Perseverance is a combination of faith and pushing through discomfort.

Your habits largely influence how successful you'll become. Effective habits result in great results. Poor habits lead to undesirable results. One of the most effective ways to take your life to the next level is to create habits that support your goals.

The most successful people in the world have the best habits for success. Pick up a couple of these habits and integrate them into your life. You'll be glad you did!

We've talked about numerous steps that will strengthen your business:

- Manage your mindset.
- Clarify the problem.
- Focus on Clients.
- Conduct a SWOT analysis.
- Create objectives and a plan.
- Reduce costs.
- Use low-cost marketing.
- Be persistent and creative.

Each of these steps requires work. You must be willing to dig into your business to figure out what isn't working. Create a clear plan of attack that you will diligently follow. You have to make hard decisions about what costs to cut and get creative with low-cost marketing.

If you take action on these things, you will dramatically increase the odds of your survival. **You will tip the scales in your favor.**

During the dark days of WWII, Winston Churchill famously urged the British people to, "...*never give in, never give in, never, never, never, never-in nothing, great or small, large or petty - never give in except to convictions of honor and good sense. Never yield to force; never yield to the apparently overwhelming might of the enemy.*"

It was that never-say-die attitude that helped Britain stay afloat in the face of incredible difficulties.

The same attitude will keep your business afloat as well. Keep moving forward. You've Got This. If you enjoyed the reading but need additional resources join our FB page at AIM motivation.

www.ingramcontent.com/pod-product-compliance
Lightning Source LLC
Chambersburg PA
CBHW050320220526
45465CB00005B/2059